The Illustrated Guide to
DOWNTOWN
PORTLAND

MAPS • INFO • PHOTOGRAPHS

First Edition

Editor/Publisher: Justin L. Gottlieb

Design/Layout: Kyla Barnott

Metro Publishing, LLC

Thank you for your participation and contributions:
City of Portland, TriMet, PGE Park, Portland Saturday Market, Powell's Bookstore, OMSI,
Pioneer Courthouse Square, Portland State University, Pioneer Place, Portland Art Museum,
Oregon Historical Society, Multnomah County Library, Rose Quarter,
Metro Regional Government, Ellen Spitaleri, Portland Center for the Performing Arts.

A photographic thank you to:
Scot Kendrick(A), Ron Hawkins(B), Shirley Johnson(C), Heather Cleveland(D),
Barbara McIntyre(E), TriMet(F), Portland Saturday Market(G), PGE Park(H),
Classical Chinese Garden(I), Port of Portland(J), and Sternwheeler Rose (K).
Unmarked photographs taken by Metro Publishing, LLC.

(All photographs are property of the individual or organization)

Printed in the United State of America
Published by Metro Publishing, LLC
Distributed by Metro Publishing, LLC
Printed by: Cenveo (GAC) 2000 NW Wilson St. Portland, OR 97209
ISBN: 0-9771504-0-2

Editor/Publisher: Justin L. Gottlieb
Layout/Designer: Kyla Barnott

Special Sales:

TAG™ guidebooks published and distributed by Metro Publishing,
LLC are available at bulk purchase rates for corporations, clubs, or
organization for sales promotions, premiums, and gifts. Special editions, including personalized covers, excerpts of existing guides, and
corporate imprints, can be created in large quantities for specific needs.
For more information contact Metro Publishing, LLC at 808 SW Third
Ave, Ste. 220, Portland, OR 97204 (503) 224-5717.

Special Note:

Every effort has been made to ensure the accuracy of the information
in this book. Please note that certain details are subject to change and
Metro Publishing, LLC cannot accept the consequences arising from
the use of this book.

TAG™ Trademark/Travel Ace Guide™ Notice are registered trade-
marks of Metro Publishing, LLC. Unauthorized use will be pursued to
the full extent of the law.

Metro Publishing, LLC
808 SW Third Ave, Ste 220
Portland, OR 97204
www.metropublish.com

♻ This publication has been printed on 10% recycled paper with soy-based inks.

From the Editor:

Welcome to Portland, Oregon!

Downtown Portland offers a wealth of activities, parks and sights that can hardly be experienced in a single trip. Our goal is to provide the most accurate and accessible information focusing on quality, ease and accessibility.

Several features set <u>TAG™ Downtown Portland</u> apart from other guides, pamphlets and magazines.

- ◆ Our guide has absolutely no advertisements.
- ◆ We utilize the most accurate maps for navigating the city. This includes a flip-out downtown map, a regional map, chapter/localized maps and sight maps.
- ◆ Included is historical information, admission pricing, and TAG™ Tips that will save you both time and money.
- ◆ Photographs create a visual sense of location so that you know when you are at your destination.
- ◆ Basic information on transportation, weather, restaurants and time allotments for specific points of interest.
- ◆ Suggested itineraries from three hours to several days.

In addition, TAG™ produces a limited number of copies in each edition so that information and photographs can be updated frequently. Your suggestions, comments, and photographs are welcome for publication consideration through our website <u>www.metropublish.com.</u>

I wish you safe and happy travels and look forward to receiving your comments and suggestions.

Sincerely,

Justin Gottlieb
Editor/Publisher

The mileage sign at Pioneer Courthouse Square.

Table of Contents

Chapter 1: The Basics

Downtown Portland is simple to navigate and with the following travel tips, you can make the most of your time, energy and resources. TAG ™ recommends utilizing the Portland Metropolitan areas mass transit system, known as TriMet. All bus lines either run through downtown Portland or connect to lines that do. If you have any questions or concerns, TriMet's bus drivers are more than willing to assist you.

Driving is also an option. TAG ™ has included the location of public parking lots and if you plan on leaving your car for the day expect to pay about $15.

Downtown Portland Post Office locations are included for your convenience.

> (i) TAG™ Safety Tip: Downtown Portland has many street people, panhandlers, and vagrants. They will repeatedly ask for money, bus fare, cigarettes, etc. No one is under any obligation to give anything. If you experience any form of harassment or threats, contact the police at 911.

> TAG™ Tip: Fareless Square provides free rides on TriMet within the downtown area. Think of it as travel between all stops within the I-405 loop and the river. Anything outside this area requires a fare.

> TAG™ Tip: Portland is accessible to people with disabilities and is wheelchair friendly. All buses, parks, and points of interest included in TAG™ have paved paths, lift systems, and ramps.

Portland City Center & Fareless Square

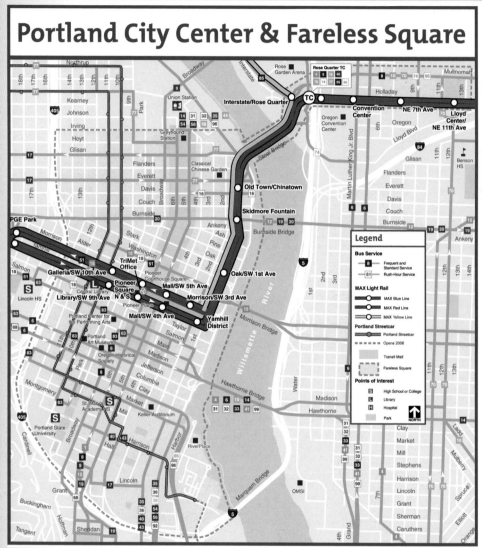

Map provided by TriMet

All-Day Ticket: About $4 buys an individual ticket valid for travel within all zones for one full day

10-Ticket Book: A book of 10 single-ride tickets costs under $20.

Children under 7 ride free with a paying passenger.

TriMet fares are valid on buses, MAX and Portland Streetcar.

TriMet
Transportation

Central Building
4017 SE 17th
Lost & Found
503.962.7655
General & Trip Information:
503.238.RIDE (7433)

Rides are free within Fareless Square, an area encompassing most of downtown Portland and the Lloyd District (within the boundaries of the Willamette River, NW Irving Street, and the I-405 freeway), as well as MAX stations from the Rose Quarter to Lloyd Center. Fare (less than $2 for an Adult All-Zone Ticket) is not required unless you are traveling outside of this area.

Fun Fact:
TriMet's transit network includes a MAX light rail system and 93 bus lines serving 575 square miles of the Portland metropolitan area.

Fun Fact:
TriMet carries more people than any other U.S. transit system of its size.

Fun Fact:
TriMet's MAX and buses combined eliminate 198,000 daily car trips, or 62 million trips each year. In all, TriMet service reduces smog-producing pollutants by about 4.2 tons every day.

Streetcar

For nearly 30 years, Portlanders have dreamed of a streetcar system.

With the creation of the Vintage Trolley system in the 1980s, Portland began to see what it could be like if small-scale trains returned to the city.

The Portland Streetcar is designed to fit the scale and traffic patterns of the neighborhoods it travels. The streetcars run in mixed traffic and, except platform stops, accommodate existing curbside parking and loading. The Portland Streetcar is owned and operated by the City of Portland.

Streetcars arrive at each marked stop approximately every 15 minutes throughout the day.

TAG ™ Tip: A one-way fare on the streetcar is $1.50. However, any TriMet fare within the allotted transfer time period is valid. No fare is necessary within the Fareless Square area.

Vintage Trolley

A round-trip on the Vintage Trolley from Lloyd Center to downtown Portland, or the reverse, takes about 45 minutes. Vintage Trolleys run on MAX tracks and make all regular MAX stops. No fare is charged and it runs on Sundays.

Parking Meters

General Parking Info:

Street parking in Portland is metered at $1.25 per hour between the hours of 8 a.m. to 7 p.m. Street parking is free on Sundays and federal holidays.

Meters can be found in the center of each block in the form of a green tower. These machines take coins (quarters, dimes, and nickels) and Credit/Debit cards. Time is purchased in 15 minute increments.

Metered spaces are marked in increments of 90 minutes, 1 hour, 2 hours, 3 hours or 5 hours (this denotes time for all spaces on that block) and times are color coded. A receipt will be given with the metered expiration time and it should be affixed to the inside of the curbside window.

Using the Meters:

1. Locate the nearest meter to your space.
2. Note time allotment and decide how long you will be occupying the space.
3. Calculate approximate cost (30¢ per 15 minutes).
4. Insert coins in marked slot and press large green button on the lower right.
5. Parking tag and receipt will be printed.
6. Affix parking tag to the inside of the curbside window. (The back of the ticket can be removed and used as an adhesive surface)

For Credit/Debit Use:
Steps 1 to 3 same as above:

4. If using Credit or Debit Card, slide card into reader with Visa/MasterCard emblem facing up and towards you.
5. Push either button above the card reader. The one to the right is "Add 15 minutes" and allows the minimum purchase of time. The left button is to "Add maximum." TAG recommends purchasing the maximum time allowed.
6. Press large green button on the lower right.
7. Pull Credit/Debit card out quickly.
8. Parking tag and receipt will be printed.
9. Affix parking tag to the inside of the inside of the curbside window. (The back of the ticket can be removed and used as an adhesive surface).

Reminder: Note time printed. If your car is still occupying a street space after the printed time, your car will be ticketed.

TAG™ Tip: Your parking sticker is valid at any space throughout the city until the printed expiration time. Remember not to exceed the maximum time limit for any block or space you move to.

i

Other Downtown Options

Garages:

Smart Park garages are owned and operated by the City of Portland

Locations:

SW 3rd & Alder: 503.823.2895
NW Naito Pkwy & Davis: 503.823.2898
SW 10th & Yamhill: 503.823.2893
SW 1st & Jefferson: 503.823.2892
SW 4th & Yamhill: 503.823.2897

TAG™ Tip: Hundreds of participating merchants will pay for your first 2 hours of parking when you spend at least $25. Remember to take your ticket with you and ask for a validation.

Taxis & Executive Towncars:

Broadway Cab Co.
503.227.1234
1734 NW 15th Ave
Portland, OR

New Rose City Cab Co.
503.282.7707
1533 NE Alberta St
Portland, OR

Classic Chauffeur
503.238.8880
540 NW 5th Ave
Portland, OR

Pioneer Executive
Towncar
503.731.8783
516 SE Morrison St # M2
Portland, OR

Radio Cab
503.227.1212
1613 NW Kearney St
Portland, OR

Portland Taxi Co.
503.256.5400
12624 NE Halsey St
Portland, OR

Regional Transportation

Airport:

Portland International Airport (PDX) is the major point of air travel for the Portland-Vancouver area. PDX provides frequent airline service to domestic destinations and significant international service to Europe and Asia.

TriMet's MAX Red Line is the first "train to the plane" on the West Coast. The ride between PDX and downtown Portland takes about 38 minutes with a cost of under $2. Trains depart approximately every 15 minutes between 5 a.m. and 11:30 p.m.

In addition, over 3,300 public parking spaces are available in the parking garage adjacent to the terminal; 1,400 long-term parking spaces are located near the terminal with an additional 7,800 economy spaces available 10 minutes from the airport.

Avis, Budget, Dollar, Enterprise, and Hertz Rent-a-Car companies are located in the terminal building. Alamo, Thrifty and National Rent-a-Car are also available and have frequent shuttle service between the airport and their rental facilities.

Portland
International
Airport (PDX)
7000 NE
Airport Way
503.460.4234
800.815.4636 TDD
1.877.739.4636

Amtrack:

Union Station provides passenger train service through Amtrak. Regular trips leave Portland heading north to Seattle and south to Los Angles. Amtrak also offers east-bound service to Chicago.

Union Station
800 NW 6th Ave.
503.273.4865

Greyhound:

Just across the street from Union Station is Portland's bus terminal. Greyhound and other bus lines offer more than 28 daily departures serving locations up and down the West Coast and to points East.

Bus Terminal
NW 6th Ave. &
Irving Street
503.243.2361
800.321.2222

Highways:

Downtown Portland is accessible by two major Interstate Highways. Both I-5 and I-84 lead into the city. I-405 provides a loop around the Westside of downtown Portland, connecting to I-5 at the Marquam Bridge and the Fremont Bridge. I-405 has accessible exits to the Central City (chapter 2), the Pearl District (page 50) and to Northwest (page 54).

13

Post Offices

Main Office
Post Office
715 NW Hoyt St
Monday to Friday
7 a.m. to 6:30 p.m.

5th Ave and Burnside
Post Office
204 SW 5th Ave
Monday to Friday
7 a.m. to 6 p.m.

University Station
Post Office
1505 SW 6th Ave
Monday to Friday
7 a.m. to 6 p.m.

Solomon Courthouse
Post Office
620 SW Main
Monday to Friday
7 a.m. to 6 p.m.

Main Post Office:
Broadway & Hoyt

General Phone Numbers

American Red Cross	503.284.1234
Auto Impound Location Info.	503.823.0044
Better Business Bureau	503.226.3981
Child Abuse Hotline (Mult. County)	503.731.3100
Consumer Complaints	503.229.5576
Humane Society (lost animals)	503.285.7722
Permit Center Information	503.823.7310
Portland Police Information (non-emergency)	503.823.3333
Women's Crisis Line	503.235.5333

Weather

The old adage in Portland is that the rain is "liquid sunshine". However, Portland boasts some of the warmest, sunniest, and nicest days in the United States during the summer months. In the summer the temperature is warm with crisp blue skies (70° F to 85° F). If you are visiting during this time of year, bring a blanket, sunglasses, and a lightweight jacket (in case of the occasional shower) and remember that outdoor activities become crowded with visitors and locals alike. It is a great time to explore the parks and the great outdoors.

The other nine months of the year bring a slow steady rain with moderate temperatures. A few days each month provide some sun but locals never count on it for more than a few hours. This makes umbrellas and raincoats a necessity and should be accessible during all seasons, especially the fall and winter. When it's raining TAG™ recommends exploring Portland's indoor activities such as OMSI, the Portland Art Museum, Powell's Bookstore, Ecotrust Building and the theater community.

Portland rarely dips below the freezing level. If it does snow, it will be in late December, January or February. These storms only tend to last a day or two.

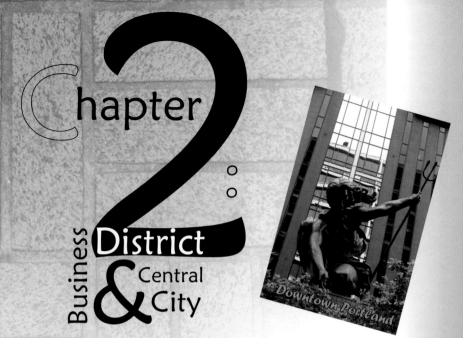

Chapter 2:
Business District & Central City

Downtown Portland

Chapter 2 covers what is commonly known as the center of Portland. Most of the cultural, economic, professional and retail activities occur in this section of the city. The following pages highlight the major points of interest in this area which include public spaces, parks, shopping, cultural sites and recreation facilities. Many of these places are free and open to the public. Examples include **Pioneer Place**, the **South Park Blocks**, **Portland State University** and **Waterfront Park**. Other points of interest such as the **Portland Art Museum**, the **Oregon Historical Society** and **PGE Park** do require admission.

TAG ™ has provided sample time allotments for each attraction. These may vary according to your level of interest, knowledge or inclement weather. In addition, websites and telephone numbers have been added as a source of additional information.

TAG™ Tip: Chapters are structured for accessible walking tours of the specific area. By following the detailed map on the next page, you can begin at any featured site and create your own tour. This allows you to make the most of your time.

TAG™ Tip: **Pioneer Square** is the heart of downtown Portland. The square contains the Visitor Information Center and a TriMet's Customer Assistance Office. This is where current and up to date information on events and activities are displayed.

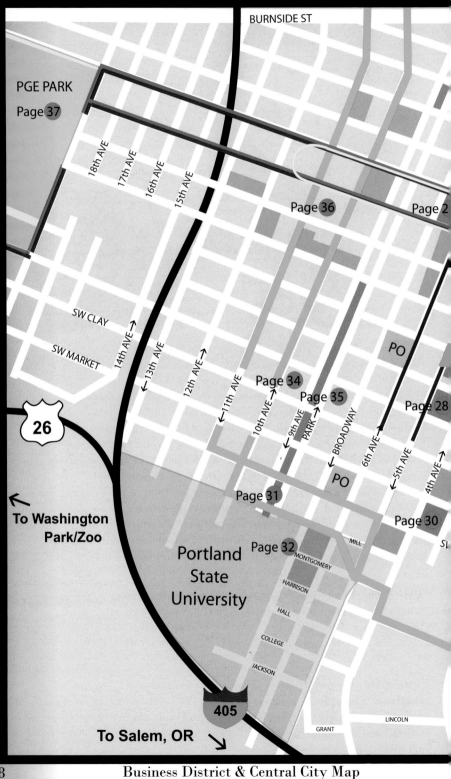

BURNSIDE ST

PGE PARK
Page 37

18th AVE
17th AVE
16th AVE
15th AVE

Page 36

Page 2

SW CLAY

SW MARKET

14th AVE
13th AVE
12th AVE
11th AVE
10th AVE
9th AVE
PARK
BROADWAY
6th AVE
5th AVE
4th AVE

Page 34

Page 35

Page 28

PO

26

Page 31

PO

Page 30

To Washington
Park/Zoo

Portland
State
University

Page 32

MONTGOMERY

MILL

HARRISON

HALL

COLLEGE

JACKSON

405

To Salem, OR

GRANT

LINCOLN

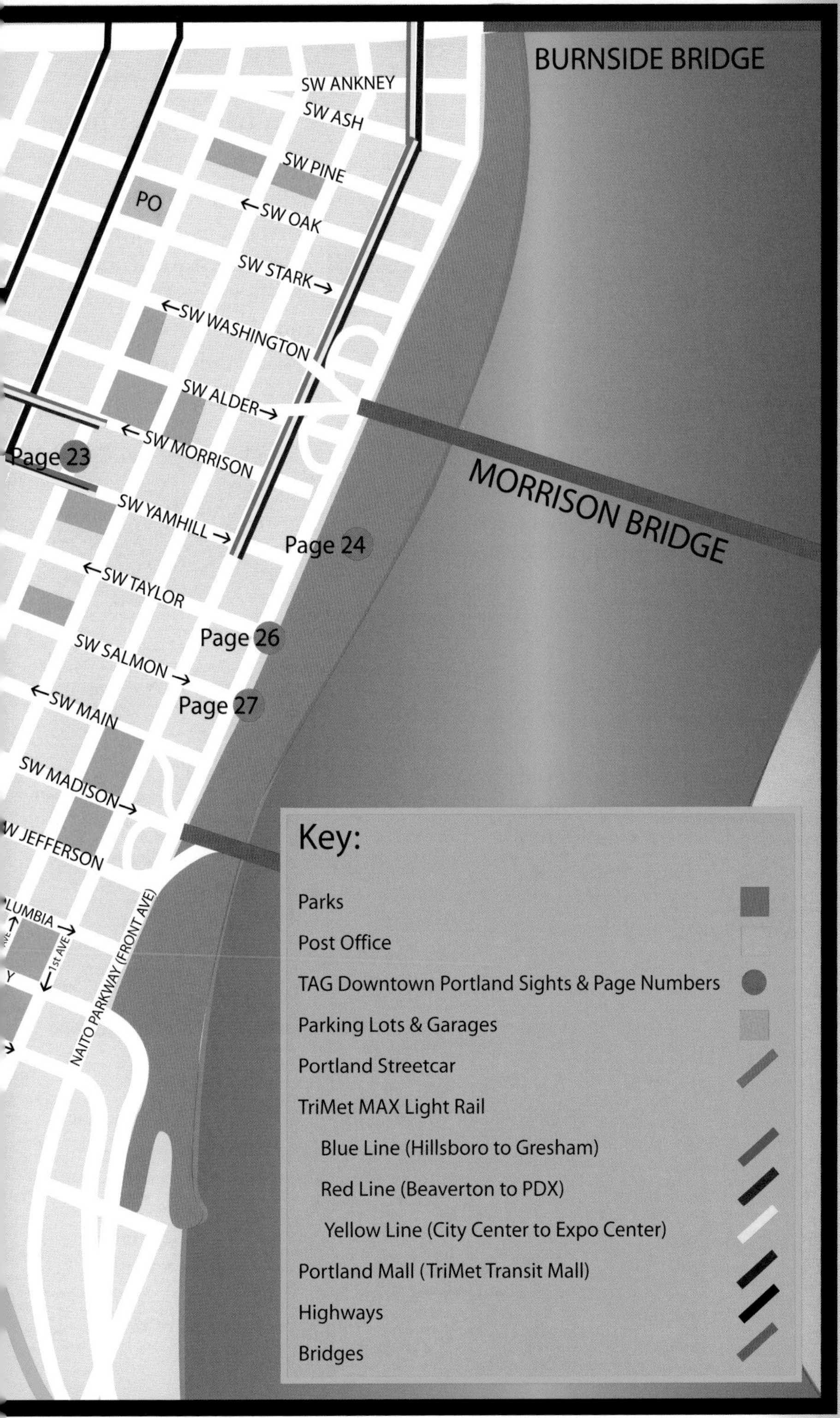

BURNSIDE BRIDGE

SW ANKNEY
SW ASH
SW PINE
PO
←SW OAK
SW STARK→
←SW WASHINGTON
SW ALDER→
← SW MORRISON
Page 23
SW YAMHILL →
Page 24
←SW TAYLOR
Page 26
SW SALMON →
←SW MAIN
Page 27
SW MADISON→

MORRISON BRIDGE

W JEFFERSON

LUMBIA

Y

NAITO PARKWAY (FRONT AVE)

1st AVE

Key:

Parks

Post Office

TAG Downtown Portland Sights & Page Numbers

Parking Lots & Garages

Portland Streetcar

TriMet MAX Light Rail

   Blue Line (Hillsboro to Gresham)

   Red Line (Beaverton to PDX)

   Yellow Line (City Center to Expo Center)

Portland Mall (TriMet Transit Mall)

Highways

Bridges

Unique Sight Features of Pioneer Courthouse Square

"Allow Me"- This Portland icon is a life-sized sculpture of a man offering his umbrella and was created by J. Seward Johnson.

Mile Post Sign: This post measures the distances to Portland's sister-cities and other unique international and geographic locations.

Weather Machine: This innovative creation consists of three weather symbols, each representing an element of Portland's typical climate. Each day at noon a musical fanfare initiates a two-minute sequence that involves the appearance of the three weather symbols: *HELIA: A stylized sun, for clear sunny days. BLUE HERON: For the days of drizzle, mist and transitional weather. DRAGON: Stormy days of heavy rain and winds.*

Waterfall Fountain: Portland celebrates its fountains, and Pioneer Courthouse Square is no exception. The central waterfall cascades down a series of large granite blocks into a reflecting pool. The fountain serves as the entry into the Visitor Information center. *Architect Will Martin designed the square and its waterfall fountain in 1983.*

Pioneer Courthouse Square

Between Morrison & Yamhill
and Broadway & Sixth
Visitors Center is open
six days a week:
Mon.-Fri., 8:30 a.m.- 5:30 p.m.;
Saturday, 10 a.m.- 4 p.m.
Closed on Sunday
503.275.8355

Time Allotment:
1-2 Hours

Travel Brief:

The space that defines the City of Portland is Pioneer Courthouse Square. The square has outgrown its namesake of Pioneer Courthouse due to its place in local lore as Portland's living room.

Pioneer Courthouse Square officially opened on April 6, 1984, exactly 133 years after the founding of Portland. The square is the heart of the city, with more than 25,000 people passing by each day, and thousands more visiting it directly. It is the single most visited public space in Oregon's largest city.

In addition, Pioneer Courthouse Square is an amazing outdoor venue. It hosts over 300 activities and events each year (that comes to almost one per day). These range from large-scale concerts to cultural festivals. Each red brick block carries a name (more than 68,000); each name symbolizes the people that make Portland such an extraordinary city.

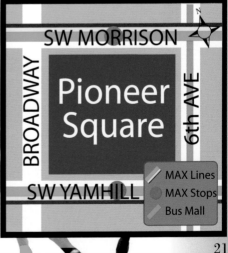

SW MORRISON

BROADWAY

Pioneer Square

6th AVE

SW YAMHILL

MAX Lines
MAX Stops
Bus Mall

(Continued on page 22)

Pioneer Courthouse Square

Pioneer Courthouse Square is home to the Visitors Association Information Area and TriMet's Customer Assistance Office. Both provide information, activities, maps and other general information about the City of Portland and the surrounding region.

Activities at the Square

Echo Chamber: Stand on the round marble stone in the center of the small amphitheater, face the steps and speak. You will be amazed by the echo you hear.

Famous Bricks: Pioneer Courthouse Square has some very special names contained within its bricks. They include John F. Kennedy, Frodo Baggins, Bruce Springsteen, John Lennon, William Shakespeare, George Washington, etc. A complete list is available at the visitors center.

Bronze Chess Boards: Resting on the fallen columns on the Morrison Street side of the Square, three bronze chess boards are available for playing chess or checkers on a first come first served basis.

Pioneer Place

Between 5th & 3rd and
Morrison & Taylor
503.228.5800
Open 7 days a week

**Time Allotment:
2-4 Hours**

Travel Brief:

Opened in 1990 and expanded in 2000, Pioneer Place stands as downtown Portland's top shopping destination for tourists and locals alike. Covering three square blocks and containing over 100 retail outlets, this mall has something for everyone.

As Portland's number one place to make a fashion statement it has 80 specialty stores and 20 national retailers anchored by Tiffany's Co. and Saks Fifth Avenue. In addition to the national names you know and love, Pioneer Place has plenty of local, one-of-a-kind shops found only in Portland, they include Twist, Moda Nova, Toy Bliss, The Living Quarters and The Fossil Cartel.

Pioneer Place contains a full-service movie theater showing the latest releases, a food court featuring over 15 food vendors offering everything from pizza to Indian cuisine. More formal restaurants are available in Todai (an all-you-can-eat Japanese restaurant) and Macaroni Grill on Third and Yamhill. With all these options you may never want to leave one of the largest downtown malls in America.

Unique Sight Features of Waterfront Park

The Founders' Stone honors Portland's founders, William Pettygrove and Asa Lovejoy, who tossed a coin to decide whether their new town would be named Boston or Portland.

In 1993, the Police Memorial, located at SW Jefferson near the Hawthorne Bridge, was dedicated to Portland police officers who gave their lives in the performance of their official duties.

The Battleship Oregon Memorial was built in 1956 to honor an 1893 ship. The U.S.S. Oregon was nicknamed "the Bulldog of the United States Navy" and fought in many battles before it was retired from service. On July 4, 1976, a time capsule was sealed in the base of the memorial and will be opened on July 5, 2076.

On August 3, 1990, the Japanese American Historical Plaza was dedicated to the memory of those who were deported to inland internment camps during World War II. In the memorial garden, artwork and poetry tell the story of the Japanese people in the Northwest – of immigration, elderly immigrants, native-born Japanese Americans, soldiers who fought in U.S. military services and the business people who worked hard and had hopes for the future.

Waterfront Park: Tom McCall

Travel Brief:

Waterfront Park was completed and dedicated in 1978, gaining instant popularity, and in 1984, the park was renamed Governor Tom McCall Waterfront Park.

In the late 1920s, a seawall was built along the Willamette's Westbank for the protection of downtown Portland from annual floods. The wall separated the people of Portland from the river. The construction of Harbor Drive along the Westbank in the 1940s continued to isolate the public from the river.

With the opening of the Eastbank Freeway (Marquam Bridge and I-5), Harbor Drive became less important for city access. In 1968, Governor Tom McCall created the Harbor Drive Task Force to study proposals for creating a public open space along this stretch. In 1974, Harbor Drive was torn up and construction of a Waterfront Park began.

www.parks.ci.portland.or.us

Between Naito Parkway & the Willamette River
From SW Harrison to NW Glisan

General Info:
Acreage: 36.59
Acquired in 1927

Time Allotment:
2-4 Hours

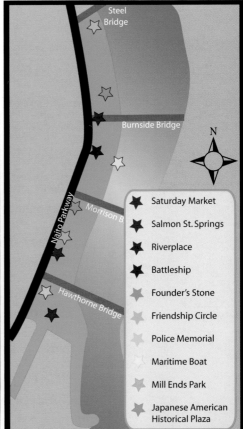

Steel Bridge

Burnside Bridge

Naito Parkway

Morrison B

Hawthorne Bridge

N

- Saturday Market
- Salmon St. Springs
- Riverplace
- Battleship
- Founder's Stone
- Friendship Circle
- Police Memorial
- Maritime Boat
- Mill Ends Park
- Japanese American Historical Plaza

Mill Ends Park

At the Intersection of SW
Naito Parkway & Taylor

General Info.
Acreage: 452 Square Inches

Time Allotment:
10 Minutes

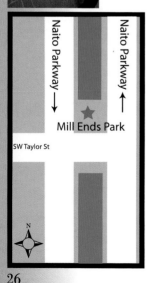

Travel Brief:

In 1946, Dick Fagan returned from World War II to resume his career with the Oregon Journal (a former daily newspaper). His office, on the second floor above Front Street, gave him a view of not only a busy street (Harbor Drive/Naito Parkway) but also an unused hole in the median. He suspected a light pole was to be placed there. When no pole arrived to fill in this hole, weeds took over the space. Fagan decided to take matters into his own hands and began to plant flowers.

Fagan wrote a popular column called Mill Ends for Oregon Journal. He used this column to describe the park and the various "events" that occurred there. Fagan billed the space as the "World's Smallest Park."

The park was dedicated on St. Patrick's Day in 1948, and Fagan continued to write about activities in and around the park until he died in 1969.

This illusive park is well-known but difficult to find. It is one of Portland's more interesting open spaces.

www.parks.ci.portland.or.us

Salmon Street Springs

B

Travel Brief:

Salmon Street Springs is at SW Salmon and Waterfront Park. This fountain celebrates city life. A computer regulates the changing patterns of the water display. At full capacity the fountain recycles 4,924 gallons of water per minute through as many as 137 jets at once. The Portland Development Commission funded the fountain and it was dedicated in 1988. A contest generated the name in 1989. The three cycles of the fountain are called Misters, Bollards and Wedding Cake.

A

TAG™ Tip: Bring a swimsuit on hot days. The fountain is a quick cool down and kids love to run through it.

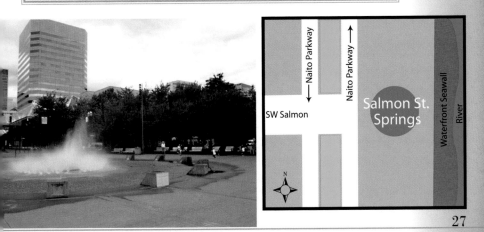

Unique Sight Features of the Plaza Blocks

Soldiers' Monument: In the center of Lownsdale Square stands the Soldiers' Monument, Douglas Tilden's monument to the Oregonians killed in the Spanish-American War. Dedicated on May 31, 1906, the tall granite obelisk is topped with a bronze replica of an infantryman of the Second Oregon U.S. Volunteer Infantry, part of the first large American fighting force ever sent overseas. At the base of this monument are two small cannons from Fort Sumter (misspelled on the plaque) brought here by Colonel Henry E. Dosch. Because the cannons were used by both Union and Confederate troops, it was Dosch's idea to face one north and one south - as they do today.

Elk Fountain: Between the two Plaza Blocks, Main Street curves around a huge elk fountain given to the city by David P. Thompson. He served as Portland's mayor from 1879-1882. One day, he looked out of the office window in his New Market Building at the Skidmore Fountain, and decided that he wanted to dedicate a fountain to the city as well.

Thompson commissioned Roland Hinton Perry, whose work adorns the Library of Congress and the dome of the Pennsylvania state capitol, to create a sculpture. In 1900, a bronze elk fountain was presented to commemorate the elk that once grazed nearby. Local architect H.G. Wright designed the stone base, which included drinking troughs for horses and dogs. Many have tried to have the elk removed because it is a traffic obstacle. Thompson's elk and the Plaza Blocks are designated as Historic Landmarks.

Plaza Blocks

SW 4th & Main
General Information
Acreage: 1.84
Acquired in 1869
Time Allotment:
1 1/2-2 Hours

Travel Brief:

The Plaza Blocks, consisting of Chapman and Lownsdale Squares, are located in downtown Portland between Third and Fourth Avenues and Salmon and Jefferson Streets.

The square between SW Main and Madison is named for former Iowa territorial legislator and native Virginian William W. Chapman (1808-1892), who arrived in Portland in 1850. An attorney with business interests, he also served as Surveyor General of Oregon. In 1870, he sold this land to the city.

The north square is named for Kentuckian Daniel H. Lownsdale, who settled in Portland in 1845 when there were fewer than 800 people in the city.

Chapman Square was originally designed for the exclusive use of women and children and features all female gingko trees, while Lownsdale Square was to be the "gentlemen's gathering place." They now coexist and men, women and children can enjoy both.

Lake Tai Rock a gift from Suzhou, China, sister city to Portland.

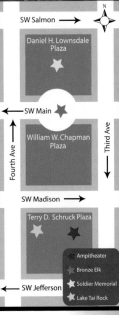

SW Salmon →

N

Daniel H. Lownsdale Plaza

← SW Main

William W. Chapman Plaza

Fourth Ave

Third Ave

SW Madison →

Terry D. Schruck Plaza

★ Ampitheater
● Bronze Elk
★ Soldier Memorial
★ Lake Tai Rock

← SW Jefferson

29

Keller Fountain Park

SW 3rd & Clay
General
Information:
Acreage 0.92
Acquired in 1968
Time Allotment:
30 Minutes

Travel Brief:

During the remodeling of the Civic Auditorium in the early 1960s, plans to create an open space across the street were being discussed. The proposal submitted by Lawrence Halprin, a well-known San Franciscan architect, was approved in 1968. Designed by Angela Danadjieva, the Forecourt Fountain, now Keller Fountain, was completed in 1970.

13,000 gallons of water per minute cascade through its terraces and platforms, suggesting the Northwest's abundant waterfalls. The concrete fountain became an instant city landmark and an internationally acclaimed open space.

Keller Auditorium

In 1978, it was renamed the Ira C. Keller Fountain in memory of the civic leader and first chairman of the Portland Development Commission. It has been said that it was Keller's enormous energy that made urban renewal work in Portland possible.

www.parks.ci.portland.or.us

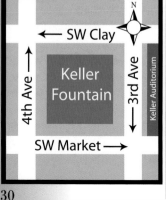

South Park Blocks

Travel Brief:

Envisioned in 1853 as a European promenade park containing 26 blocks covered with fir trees, the park has remained true to its nature. However, in the ensuing 150 years, only 12 of the blocks were constructed into what is now the South Park Blocks.

Consensus abounds in Portland that this space should remain "a cathedral of trees with a simple floor of grass". Residents appreciate this because the grass floor is perfect for picnics, a game of frisbee, and just enjoying the outdoors.

The South Park Blocks are adjacent to the Portland Art Museum, the Oregon Historical Society and Schnitzer Auditorium.

An entire day can be spent exploring the different facets of the park. In addition, the block between Main street and Madison street is known as Lincoln Square. Standing 10-feet tall is a bronze statue of Abraham Lincoln. His bowed head gives the park a quiet dignity invoking the integrity of a great man.

Rebecca At The Well/Shemanski Fountain located between SW Salmon and Main. This Italianesque fountain was a gift to the city from Joseph Shemanski in 1926. The Regional Arts and Culture Council partnered with the Water Bureau to restore this fountain in 2004.

D

SW Salmon

★ ☆

SW Main

☆

SW Madison

★

SW 9th Ave

SW Jefferson

SW Park

☆

SW Columbia

SW Clay

SW Market

★ Theodore Roosevelt
★ Shemanski Fountain
☆ Lincoln Square
☆ Simon Benson Memorial
★ Peace Plaza

N

SW Mill

31

Unique Sight Features of PSU

Lincoln Hall was originally Portland School District's Lincoln High School and was constructed in 1911. The building now houses the School of Fine and Performing Arts where classes, concerts, workshops and performances take place almost daily.

1620 SW Park Ave.

1803 SW Park Ave.

The jewel of Portland State University's campus is the Simon Benson House. The 105 year-old Queen Anne style home was moved to the campus on January 16, 2000, and restored to its original splendor. Now home to the PSU Alumni Association and a University visitors' center, the Benson House serves as a meeting place and resource center for both campus and community. The Simon Benson House is open to the public 9 a.m. to 5 p.m. Monday - Friday.

Portland Farmers Market

Best time of year is from April to October

Portland has numerous public markets located throughout the city. The markets help forge a connection between urban shoppers and farmers. All the food is produced locally and the fruits and vegetables make great snacks for the intrepid traveler.

South Park Blocks (PSU-SW Harrison &Montgomery)
Saturdays: 8:30 a.m. to 2 p.m.
Behind the Schnitzer (SW Salmon & Main)
Wednesdays: 10 a.m. to 2 p.m.
Ecotrust Parking Lot (NW Irving & Johnson)
Thursdays: 4 p.m. to 8 p.m.

TAG™ Tip: Chefs and cookbook authors demonstrate seasonal recipes Saturdays at 10 a.m. & Thursdays at 6 p.m.

www.portlandfarmersmarket.org

Portland State University

Portland State University
Campus starts at
SW Park & Market
503.725.3000

Time Allotment:
1-2 Hours

Travel Brief:

Portland State University, located along the tree-lined South Park Blocks of downtown Portland, is Oregon's only urban university and is the largest and most diverse in the state system. Its 47-acres contain over 50 buildings on a greenway for pedestrians and bicyclists which is integrated into the local community of residences and businesses.

The University District is home to labs, classrooms, offices, retail, housing and childcare facilities. The campus buildings range from the 105 year-old historic Simon Benson House to the Native American Student and Community Center completed in 2003.

Portland State started as the Vanport Extension Center in 1946. On May 30, 1948, the city of Vanport, including the Extension Center, was washed away in a devastating flood. The Center moved to Swan Island and then downtown. In September 1952, 1,272 students enrolled in their new college which had one building, Lincoln Hall. The building still stands today at the intersection of SW Market and Broadway.

www.pdx.edu

Portland Art Museum

1219 SW Park Ave
503.226.2811
Hours:
Tue-Wed, Sat 10 a.m.-5 p.m.
Thu-Fri 10 a.m.-8 p.m.
Sun 12 p.m.-5 p.m.

Time Allotment:
2-4 Hours

Travel Brief:

One of the seven oldest museums in the United States, the Portland Art Museum is internationally recognized for its permanent collection. It has the goal of giving the community a first-class museum that is accessible to all citizens. Providing weekly lectures and traveling exhibits at a reasonable cost, the campus houses a permanent collection of 35,000 objects displayed in 112,000 square feet of gallery space. Some of the Museum's notable collections are for French paintings, English silver, and artifacts from North America. The Museum also contains a graphic arts collection and a center devoted to artists of the Pacific Northwest. There is rental space available for private functions and special events occur on a weekly basis.

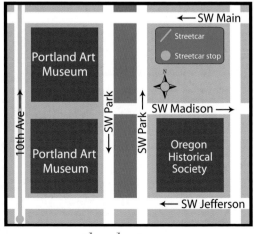

Admission:
Adults: $10
Students/Seniors: $9
Youth: $6
(6 to 18 years)
Children: Free
(4 years and under)
(Additional charges may apply for special exhibits)

www.portlandartmuseum.org

34

Oregon Historical Society

1200 SW Park Avenue
503.222.1741
Hours:
Monday through Saturday,
10 a.m. to 5 p.m.
Sunday, 12 p.m. to 5 p.m.

Time Allotment:
2-4 Hours

Travel Brief:

The Oregon Historical Society was founded in 1898. The Society opened its first office and museum in Portland City Hall and began to develop a regional research library and a collection of historical artifacts. In 1917, the Society moved into Portland's Public Auditorium (now Keller Auditorium), and in 1966 moved in to its current location on SW Jefferson and Park.

The journal of record, *Oregon Historical Quarterly*, has been published by the Society continuously since 1900. Over 150 books on Oregon history, politics and culture, as well as biographies, field guides and exhibit catalogs, have been published by the organization since 1929.

The society's collection comprises over 85,000 items which includes ancient objects from the earliest settlements illustrating the exploration of the Oregon Territory, the growth of business and industry, the development of artwork and crafts, maritime history and other Oregon related topics.

The Research Library contains one of the most extensive collections of state history materials. It includes approximately 25,000 maps, 30,000 books, 8.5 million feet of film and videotape, 16,000 rolls of microfilm and 12,000 linear feet of documents. The Research Library's photographic archives include over 2.5 million images from pre-statehood to the present day.

Admission:
Adults: $10
Students/Seniors: $8
Youth: $5
(6 to 18 years)
Children: Free
(5 years and under)
(Additional charges may apply for special exhibits)

www.ohs.org

Central Library

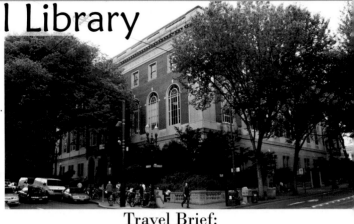

Multnomah County
Central Library
801 SW 10th Ave.
503.988.5123
Hours:
Monday: 10 a.m. to 6 p.m.
Tuesday & Wednesday:
10 a.m. to 8 p.m.
Thursday-Saturday:
10 a.m. to 6 p.m.
Sunday: 12 p.m. to 5 p.m.

Time Allotment:
2-6 Hours

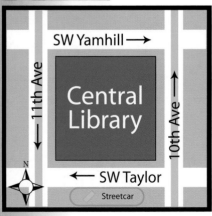

Travel Brief:

The Multnomah County Library dates its existence to 1864. Its roots are credited to a small group of Portland citizens who established a subscription library and reading room, organizing under the name "Library Association of Portland."

On March 10, 1902, the library became a tax-supported free public library, open to all residents of the city. In 1903, services were extended to all residents of Multnomah County, and the Multnomah County commissioners became ex-officio members of the library board.

The Central Library in Portland was opened in September of 1913. Designed by architect A.E. Doyle, the building took two years to build at a cost of $480,000. The Central Library building, now on the National Register of Historic Places, continues to be the heart of what has become a nationally renowned public library system.

The Historic Central Library in Portland, reopened April 8, 1997, after being closed for an extensive $24.6 million renovation that lasted two years. During the renovation period, Central Library materials (over 875 tons of them: books, magazines, reference and multimedia materials to name a few) were relocated to a temporary rented space called TransCentral Library.

www.multcolib.org

PGE Park

1844 SW Morrison St

For all PGE ticket
information call
503.553.5555
General Information:
503.553.5400

Time Allotment:
1-6 Hours

H

Travel Brief:

Historic PGE Park, a 20,000-seat, multipurpose facility located in Portland, is home to the Portland Beavers, the Portland Timbers, Portland State University football and other top sporting and entertainment events each year.

Originally constructed in 1926, PGE Park (formerly Multnomah Stadium and Civic Stadium) has undergone a number of transformations over the years, most recently a $38.5 million renovation. The refurbishment included the addition of several pavilions and field suites, a new playing surface and a seven-story manual scoreboard.

Since 2001, PGE Park has attracted several large-scale events, including a sold-out Seattle Mariners exhibition game in 2002 and a series of doubleheader soccer events for the 2003 FIFA Women's World Cup. The stadium also hosted a WUSA All-Star Game, a Seattle Seahawks intrasquad event, and an exhibition soccer match featuring the gold-medal winning U.S. Women's National Team.

Historically speaking, the stadium has a storied past that has featured presidential visits, the NFL's first game decided by overtime, an Elvis Presley concert and Soccer Bowl '77, which featured soccer legend Pele.

NW Pearl Chinatown

Chapter 3:

Greetings From Northwest

The area north of Burnside contains one of Portland's newest neighborhoods, one of its oldest neighborhoods and a cultural area.

Chinatown is home to Portland's Chinese community and has a rich and unique history in Portland. **Chinatown** provides ample Chinese restaurants and sights that can be enjoyed in a relaxed urban setting.

On Saturdays and Sundays during the summer the area east of Chinatown hosts **Portland's Saturday Market** which is a local arts and crafts market. The market is the place to purchase one of a kind gifts and souvenirs that represent the creative talent, energy and inspiration of Portland.

The **Pearl District** and **Brewery Blocks** were envisioned in the early 1990's as lifestyle neighborhoods. These areas have become trend setters in lifestyle living with million dollar condominiums, fine dining, and a plethora of upscale boutique shops. These neighborhoods are reminiscent of New York City's 5th Avenue mixed with a healthy dose of SoHo.

Northwest Portland is the bohemian center of Portland. With small boutique stores, unique restaurants, bars, and coffee shops it is the perfect area to stroll aimlessly.

Soak up life and culture in these unique Portland neighborhoods.

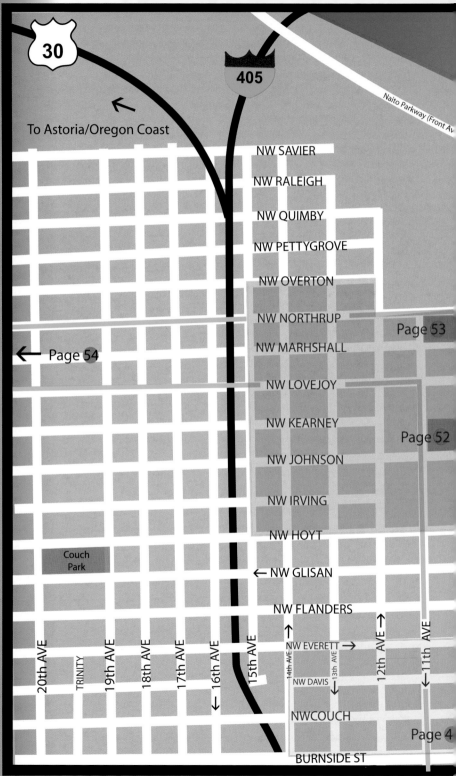

30

405

Naito Parkway (Front Av)

To Astoria/Oregon Coast

NW SAVIER

NW RALEIGH

NW QUIMBY

NW PETTYGROVE

NW OVERTON

NW NORTHRUP

Page 53

← Page 54

NW MARHSHALL

NW LOVEJOY

NW KEARNEY

Page 52

NW JOHNSON

NW IRVING

NW HOYT

Couch Park

← NW GLISAN

NW FLANDERS

20th AVE

TRINITY

19th AVE

18th AVE

17th AVE

16th AVE

15th AVE

14th AVE

NW EVERETT →

13th AVE

12th AVE

11th AVE

NW DAVIS

NWCOUCH

Page 4

BURNSIDE ST

Pearl, Northwest & Chinatown Map

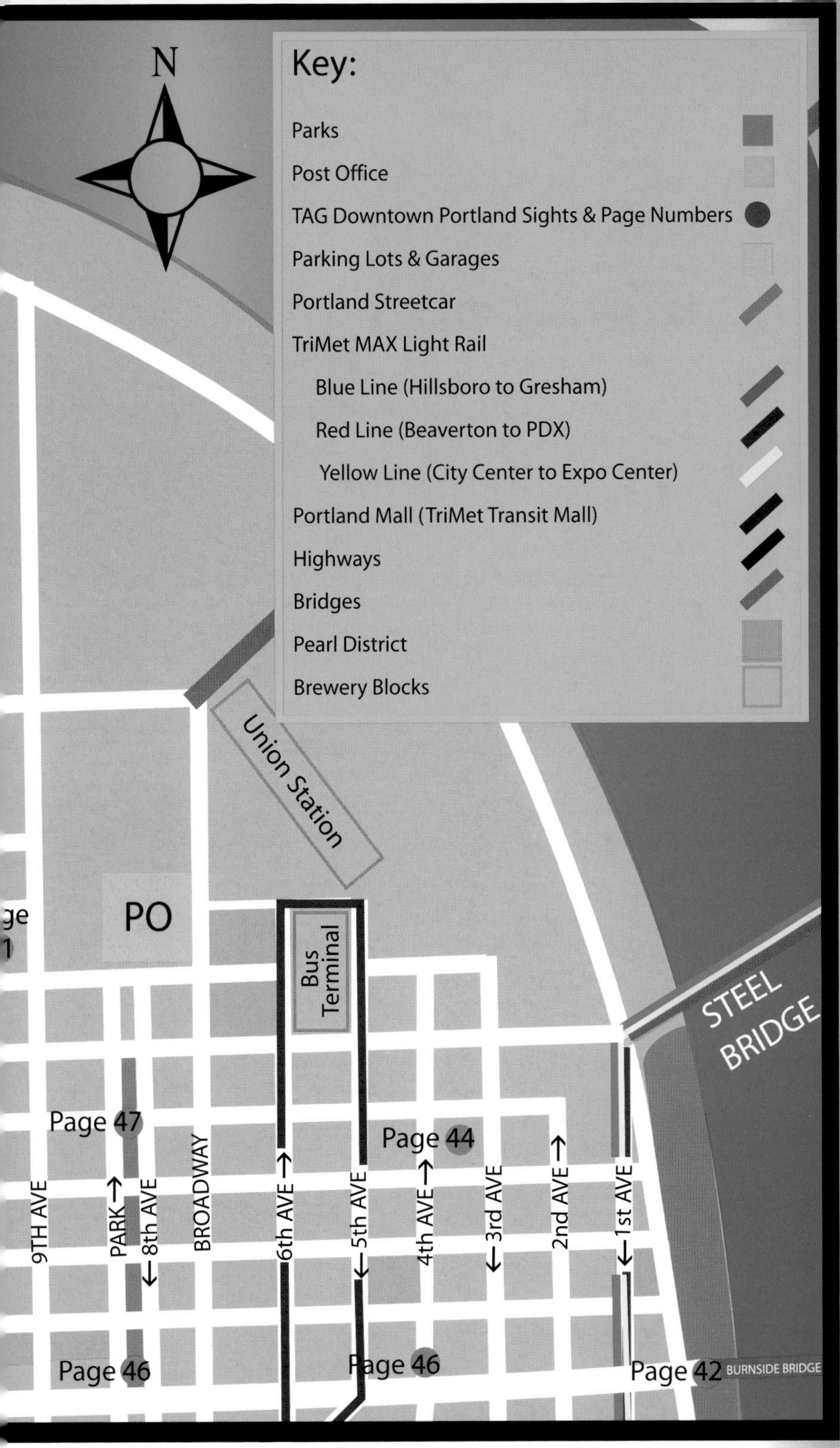

N

Key:

Parks

Post Office

TAG Downtown Portland Sights & Page Numbers ●

Parking Lots & Garages

Portland Streetcar

TriMet MAX Light Rail

   Blue Line (Hillsboro to Gresham)

   Red Line (Beaverton to PDX)

   Yellow Line (City Center to Expo Center)

Portland Mall (TriMet Transit Mall)

Highways

Bridges

Pearl District

Brewery Blocks

Union Station

ge
1

PO

Bus Terminal

STEEL BRIDGE

Page 47

Page 44

9TH AVE

PARK ↑

8th AVE ↓

BROADWAY

6th AVE ↑

5th AVE ↓

4th AVE ↑

3rd AVE ↓

2nd AVE ↑

1st AVE ↓

Page 46

Page 46

Page 42 BURNSIDE BRIDGE

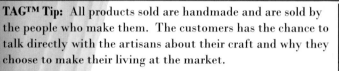

Fun Fact: Portland Saturday Market has over 400 members and generates an estimated $8 million in gross sales annually. It has become an economic engine for the historic Old Town/Chinatown neighborhood, and attracts an estimated 1 million visitors to this area each year.

*Figures provided by Portland Saturday Market

TAG™ Tip: All products sold are handmade and are sold by the people who make them. The customers has the chance to talk directly with the artisans about their craft and why they choose to make their living at the market.

Skidmore Fountain

Travel Brief:

Marking the center of Portland in 1888, the fountain is a prized possession and city landmark. Stephen Skidmore, a druggist who arrived in Portland by covered wagon, left $5,000 in his will for a fountain for men, horses and dogs. His friends raised additional funds to commission a design by Olin Warner. It is inscribed

"Good Citizens Are The Riches Of A City," a quote from C. S. Wood. This has become the informal motto for the City of Portland. The fountain is Portland's oldest piece of public art and a gathering spot for locals and visitors.

Fun Fact: Portland's good citizens have created 95 neighborhood organizations and have one of the highest levels of citizen participation in the United States, with over 25,000 people participating every year.

*Figures provided by City of Portland, Office of Neighborhood Involvement

Portland Saturday Market

Underneath the Burnside
Bridge on First Ave.
Saturdays: 10 a.m. - 5 p.m.
Sundays: 11 a.m. -4:30 p.m.
Portland Saturday
Market Season:
March through Dec. 24th
Admission:
FREE
Time Allotment:
Half a Day to
a Full Day

Travel Brief:

Every Saturday and Sunday, from March until December, the Old Town/Chinatown neighborhood transforms into a thriving arts and crafts marketplace. You will be surprised at all of the elements that lie at the heart of this unusual non-profit operation.

Portland Saturday Market was the brainchild of two women, Sheri Teasdale and Andrea Scharf. Both were artists living in the area who had sold at the Saturday Market in Eugene, Oregon; their idea was to create a similar style of market for Portland.

TAG™ Tip: Every first Sunday of the month features kids activities!

Beginning in 1973, Teasdale and Scharf began to sell the idea of an open air market for arts and crafts. As a win-win situation, the artists would have an economic outlet for their work, customers would gain better access to locally-produced items, and the city would have a new attraction. The market moved to its current site under the Burnside Bridge in 1976.

Portland Saturday Market was envisioned as a market where craftspeople would share the cost of running the market collectively and would keep whatever profit they personally made. It is a market for the members, governed by the members.

NW Couch
Burnside St
SW Ankeny
SW Ash
2nd Ave
Naito Parkway
N

Portland Saturday Market
Burnside Bridge

★ Portland Saturday Market
(Under the Burnside Bridge)

★ Skidmore Fountain

// MAX lines

Unique Sight Features of the Classical Chinese Garden

These five elements give balance to the relationship between humanity and nature within the garden.

WATER: The 8,000 square feet of Zither Lake provides the unifying center for all the gardens elements. In addition, it creates a sense of infinity as the water disappears under bridges and buildings. Reflections on the water add new and unique dimensions to the beauty of the garden.

STONE: Over 500 tons of stone create a waterfall mountain, slender notched bamboo stones, and pebble stone mosaic patterns. These stone features produce visual, tactile, and symbolic relationships that tie the garden together.

POETRY: Poetic phases and lines can be found on rocks, screen panels, gateways and pillars. Literary inscriptions are an essential element of a Chinese Garden utilizing rich metaphors and allusions. They highlight the aesthetic experience and symbolic meaning of different objects and settings.

ARCHITECTURE: The nine buildings form a synergy with the surrounding landscape. Unique windows frame and focus views both within and without. Contained in the roof tiles are symbols of life's five blessings: Love of Virtue, Health, Wealth, Long Life, and Happy Endings.

PLANTS: There are more than 500 species of plants and trees, including different varieties of bamboo, rare perennials, water plants, and orchids. According to the Chinese tradition, plants are selected for both their natural grace and symbolism.

Classical Chinese Garden

NW 3rd & Everett
503.228.8131

Hours:
Open Daily
Nov-March:
10 a.m. to 5 p.m.
April-Oct:
9 a.m. to 6 p.m.

Time Allotment:
2-4 Hours

Admission:
Adults $7
Students $5.50
Seniors $6

Travel Brief:

The Classical Chinese Garden nurtures and inspires all who visit. Strolling through the garden, you will be immersed in an environment that represents the ideal landscape in miniature. The imagination will see mountains, lakes and trees that create a subtle *qi* (energy) that help everyone better understand their place within nature.

The garden changes by season, unfolding before our eyes. It is home to rare and unusual plants, nearly 100 specimen of trees, water plants, bamboo and orchids that can be enjoyed at any time of year.

Every Classical Chinese Garden incorporates five elements: stone, water, architecture, poetry, and plants to achieve the duality of nature through yin and yang.

← NW Flanders

3rd Ave

Classical
Chinese
Garden

2nd Ave

NW Everett →

N

www.portlandchinesegarden.org

45

Bronze Elephants

Travel Brief:

Da Tung (Universal Peace): Standing 12-feet high, two bronze elephants mark the entrance to the North Park Blocks at Burnside. Installed in 2002, this public piece of art is a replica of a Chinese antique dating from the late Shang Dynasty (1200-1100 BC). The elephant is embellished with figures from ancient Chinese mythology, and carries a baby elephant, Xiang Bao Bao (Baby Elephant), symbolizing that offspring shall be safe and prosperous. The statue was a gift by Chinese businessman Huo Baozhu to the City of Portland. Huo's foundry is in Xi'an, China.

The playground in the North Park Blocks.

Chinese Gate Located on 4th Ave, off Burnside.

Dedicated November 8, 1986, Portland's Chinese Gate stands as one of the most colorful and largest gates in the U.S. Upon arrival from Taiwan, R.O.C., to Portland, it took a week to assemble and has been the gateway to Chinatown ever since. Sculpted by Sun Chau.

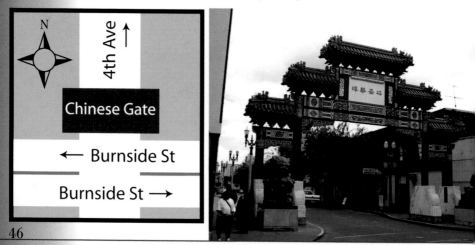

North Park Blocks

Ankeny to Glisan between
SW Park and 8th

Time Allotment:
1-2 Hours

Travel Brief:

This area is one of the original public spaces for the City of Portland. The park was dedicated in 1869 by Captain John Couch (a Portland founding father). By 1880 it was a promenade park and residential community with modest one- and two-story houses lining the blocks. Light industrial businesses, hotels, and railroad facilities moved in and created the atmosphere that still exists today.

As the North Park Blocks entered the 21st century, they have returned to their residential roots. As the Pearl District expands, the Park Blocks have become a hub of a growing residential neighborhood. In 1993, a new playground was built and is very popular among young Portlanders.

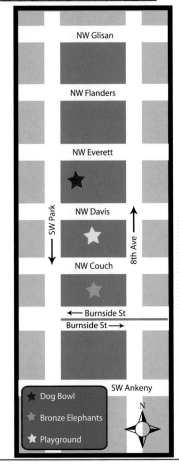

Portland Dog Bowl: This fountain was installed in 2002 and is a quirky feature of the North Park Blocks. The Dog Bowl was designed by weimaraner dog photographer William Wegman. An 8 x 10 foot patch of linoleum floor with a dog bowl on the side is a must-stop for Portland's four-legged friends. When interviewed about the design concept, Wegman stated, "If it didn't work for the dogs, it wouldn't work for me."

www.parks.ci.portland.or.us

Store Description:

Powell's City of Books is a book lover's paradise. It is considered one of, if not, the largest bookstore in the world and occupies an entire city block. It contains more than a million new and used books.

Nine color-coded rooms house over 3,500 different sections, offering something for everyone, including an incredible selection of out-of-print and hard-to-find titles.

The Rare Book Room gathers autographed first editions and other collectible volumes for readers in search of a one-of-a-kind treasure.

Every day at the buyers' counter in the Orange Room, Powell's purchases thousands of used books from the public. In addition, Powell's purchases special collections, libraries, and bookstore inventories.

www.powells.com

Facts about the City of Books:

❖ 68,000 square feet packed with books

❖ Powell's purchases 3,000 used books over the counter every day

❖ Approximately 3,000 people walk in and buy something every day

❖ Another 3,000 people just browse and drink coffee

❖ Powell's stocks 122 major subject areas and more than 3,500 subsections

❖ You'll find more than 1,000,000 volumes on Powell's shelves

❖ 65% of the stock at Powell's is used books.

So is Powell's the world's largest bookstore? Heck, it may be bigger than your whole town.

POWELL'S BOOKS

USED & NEW BOOKS

Powell's Bookstore

1005 W. Burnside
503.228.4651
Time Allotment:
Browsing the Books
2-4 Hours

Travel Brief:

In 1971, on a corner of northwest Portland, Powell's Books was founded and it has since grown into one of the world's largest bookstores. With seven locations in the Portland metropolitan area, and a successful online bookstore (www.powells.com), Powell's serves customers worldwide.

Powell's roots began in Chicago, where Michael Powell, as a University of Chicago graduate student, opened his first bookstore in 1970. Encouraged by friends and professors, including novelist Saul Bellow, Michael borrowed $3,000 to assume a lease on a bookstore in Chicago.

Michael's father Walter, a retired painting contractor, worked one summer with Michael at the Chicago bookstore. He enjoyed his experience so much that upon returning to Portland he opened his own store.

Walter Powell opened Powell's bookstore in 1971 and proceeded to buy every marketable new and used book he could find. After growing out of two smaller locations on West Burnside, Walter finally pushed his store into a former car dealership on NW 10th & Burnside, which, after many changes, remains the Powell's flagship to this day.

Michael returned to Portland in 1979 and joined Walter in building the bookstore we know today. Their unique recipe, though viewed as unorthodox, worked: used and new books, hardcover and paperback, all on the same shelf, open 365 days a year and staffed by knowledgeable and dedicated book lovers. It has become a Portland landmark and one of the citys' greatest assets.

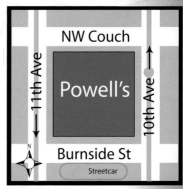

NW Couch

11th Ave

Powell's

10th Ave

Burnside St

Streetcar

Brewery Blocks

Travel Brief:

Located at the former site of the Blitz-Weinhard Brewery, the Brewery Blocks are five-square blocks located in the vibrant, post-industrial neighborhood known as the Pearl District.

This area provides an urban gateway between the Central Business District and the Pearl District. Contained within this small area are approximately 1.7 million square feet of urban retail, office space, and residential housing.

The development project ensured historic preservation of the Weinhard Brewhouse and the Armory Building. The unique aura of the area has increased retail and commercial activity, transforming it into a bustling urban neighborhood.

The design and construction of all its buildings are consistent with "environmentally friendly" sustainable development concepts. The Brewery Blocks are livable and usable spaces that will serve the community for years to come.

www.breweryblocks.com

Pearl District

Travel Brief:

A neighborhood that sprouted from an industrial wasteland into a thriving community. Many buildings in the Pearl have utilized the existing architecture to create the neighborhood we know today.

Thomas Augustine, a local gallery owner, coined the phrase "Pearl District" more than 10 years ago. His idea was to suggest that the buildings in the warehouse district were like crusty oysters, and that the galleries and artists' lofts within were like pearls.

Currently, the Pearl is home to some of Portland's finest restaurants, shops, fine art galleries, and million dollar condos. If you are looking for a night out, this is the place to see and be seen.

www.shopthepearl.com

EcoTrust Building

Jean Vollum Natural
Capital Center
721 NW 9ᵗʰ
503.227.6225

Time Allotment:
2-3 Hours

Travel Brief:

Originally constructed as a warehouse in 1895, the Natural Capital Center building was acquired by Ecotrust in 1998. An extraordinary gift from philanthropist and founding board member Jean Vollum helped create one of Portland's first environmentally friendly buildings.

The Center has gained recognition as an important contribution to the city's landscape. It showcases a unique blend of environmental innovation, historic restoration and economic vitality.

The 70,000 square foot building also houses Ecotrust's headquarters, a mix of non-profits and business tenants that are gathered around the themes of sustainable forestry and fisheries, green building, and financial investment. Visitors and the general public are welcome to explore the building and environmental exhibits. The Center features outdoor seating, a public atrium, a resource center, and an outdoor terrace with a fireplace.

Ecotrust's renovation of the brick and timber building respects the character of the original 1895 structure, while incorporating environmentally-innovative materials and techniques. The redevelopment contractor, Walsh Construction, has estimated that more than 98 percent of the construction waste has been recycled or reclaimed. The building also features an "ecoroof" that, together with street-level landscaping, filters and absorbs most, if not all, of the site's rainwater, eliminating runoff to the Willamette River.

www.ecotrust.org

Jamison Square

Between NW 10th and 11th and
NW Johnson & Kearney
General Info: Acreage: 0.96
Acquired in 2000.

Time Allotment:
1-2 Hours

Travel Brief:

The City of Portland is world renowned for its commitment to parks and open spaces. In the early 1990's, when construction of the Pearl District commenced, including open space was a non-negotiable element in the plan for both the neighborhood and the city. Jamison Square is the first of what will be several new parks between 10th and 11th Avenues in the Pearl District.

Located between NW Johnson and Kearney, it is named in honor of William Jamison, who was an exceptional person in his ability to

influence and connect with a wide variety of people. His personal magnetism, in addition to the size and scope of his art gallery, drew many people into the Pearl District. He helped make the area what it is today, a thriving community of businesses, condominiums and people who share a love for urban living.

The focal point of the park is a fountain which simulates a shallow tidal pool. Water cascades from stone joints into low pools, as the fountain continuously recirculates water with energy efficient pumps and motors.

Tanner Springs

Between NW 10th and 11th and
NW Marshall & Northrup

General Info: Acreage: 0.96
Acquired in 2005

Time Allotment:
1-2 Hours

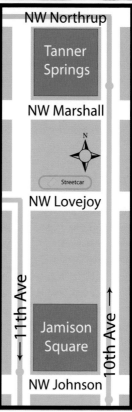

Travel Brief:

The second park developed for the Pearl District opened in August 2005. Tanner Springs Park was envisioned as a quiet and contemplative area for visitors and residents.

Designed by German landscape architect and artist Herbert Dreiseitl, Tanner Springs Park is an abstract wetland. It is reflective of the historical Couch Lake and wetland which originally filled the area between Tanner Creek and the Willamette River. The new park can be interpreted as the "pulling-back of the industrial urban fabric of the city to reveal the natural landscape that once existed at the site."

The design and development of Tanner Springs Park was made possible through funds granted to the River District Urban Renewal Area and managed by Portland Development Commission.

www.parks.ci.portland.or.us

NW Northrup

Tanner
Springs

NW Marshall

N

Streetcar

NW Lovejoy

11th Ave

Jamison
Square

10th Ave →

NW Johnson

TAG™ Tip: The area is a quick streetcar ride from downtown or the Pearl. However, good walking shoes are essential as the neighborhood is best explored by foot. Northwest's street layout is a grid and easy to navigate.

P
2
HOURS

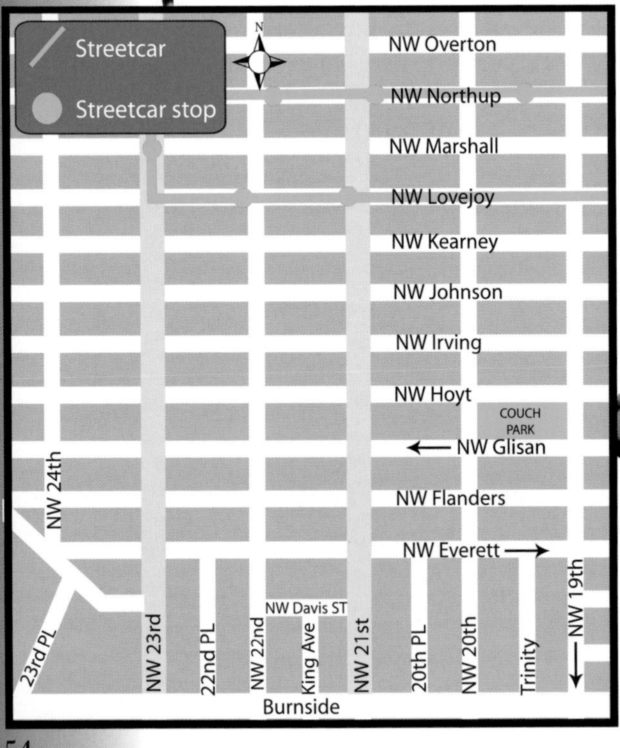
Streetcar
Streetcar stop
N
NW Overton
NW Northup
NW Marshall
NW Lovejoy
NW Kearney
NW Johnson
NW Irving
NW Hoyt
COUCH PARK
NW Glisan
NW Flanders
NW Everett
NW Davis ST
NW 24th
23rd PL
NW 23rd
22nd PL
NW 22nd
King Ave
NW 21st
20th PL
NW 20th
Trinity
NW 19th
Burnside

Northwest-Nobb Hill

Travel Brief:

A destination for shoppers searching for a unique experience, Northwest Portland otherwise known as Nobb Hill is for sophisticated shopping and fine dining.

An old Portland neighborhood where Victorian homes share the streets with boutique shops and quaint housing is perfect for an afternoon stroll.

21st and 23rd streets form the core of the shopping district with specialty and boutique stores that showcase fashion trends, unique cuisine, and fine art. In addition, Oregon microbrews, multiple coffee shops, art galleries and antique stores offer a little something for everyone.

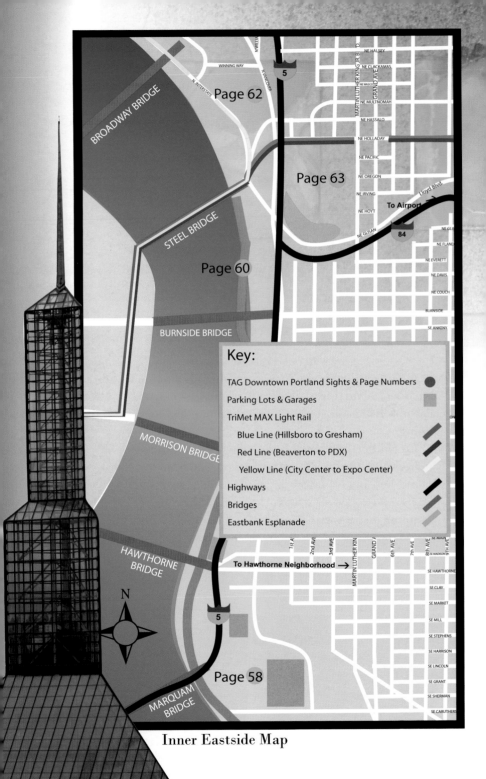

Page 62

Page 63

Page 60

Page 58

Inner Eastside Map

Key:

TAG Downtown Portland Sights & Page Numbers

Parking Lots & Garages

TriMet MAX Light Rail

   Blue Line (Hillsboro to Gresham)

   Red Line (Beaverton to PDX)

   Yellow Line (City Center to Expo Center)

Highways

Bridges

Eastbank Esplanade

To Hawthorne Neighborhood →

To Airport

BROADWAY BRIDGE

STEEL BRIDGE

BURNSIDE BRIDGE

MORRISON BRIDGE

HAWTHORNE BRIDGE

MARQUAM BRIDGE

N

WINNING WAY

N INTERSTATE

N WILLIAMS

N VANCOUVER

MARTIN LUTHER KING JR BLVD

GRAND AVE

Lloyd Blvd

NE HALSEY

NE CLACKAMAS

NE WASCO

NE MULTNOMAH

NE HASSALO

NE HOLLADAY

NE PACIFIC

NE OREGON

NE IRVING

NE HOYT

NE GLISAN

NE FLANDERS

NE EVERETT

NE DAVIS

NE COUCH

BURNSIDE

SE ANKENY

SE HAWTHORNE

SE CLAY

SE MARKET

SE MILL

SE STEPHENS

SE HARRISON

SE LINCOLN

SE GRANT

SE SHERMAN

SE CARUTHERS

1st AVE

2nd AVE

3rd AVE

MARTIN LUTHER KING

GRAND A

6th AVE

7th AVE

8th AVE

SE MAIN

SE MADISON

Chapter 4:
Inner
Eastside

The Eastbank of the Willamette River is a stark contrast to the hustle, bustle and commerce of the Westside of downtown Portland. The Eastside provides recreation, tranquility and educational activities that stimulate both the mind and body in a way that is quintessentially Portland.

Begin your exploration of the Eastside at **OMSI**: Oregon's Museum of Science and Industry. After touring **OMSI**, head North for a refreshing walk along the **Eastbank Esplanade**.

The rounded stadium at the intersection of Interstate 5 and the Steel Bridge is the **Rose Quarter**. This stadium complex contains both the **Rose Garden** and **Memorial Coliseum** which host Portland's sporting activities, concerts and large venue activities.

The two glass pillars located at the **Oregon Convention Center** define the Inner Eastside skyline. The Convention Center is one of the West Coast's largest and most beautiful facilities hosting different events and activities almost every weekend.

Unique Sight Features of OMSI

<u>Kendall Planetarium</u> —$5.50 (Adult & Youth)
 A 52-foot domed theater thrills both long-time star gazers and the budding astronomer. Using state-of-the-art technologies, the experience focuses on astronomy and space science to enhance our understanding of how Earth relates to the surrounding universe.

<u>OMNIMAX</u> — $8.50 (Adult) $6.50 (Youth)
 With a five-story domed screen and 30-degree, stadium seating, the OMNIMAX® Dome Theater is a cinematic experience unlike any other. The large-format image (ten times the size of standard 35mm film) and surround-sound put you in the center of the action.

<u>U.S.S. Blueback (SS 581)</u> —$5.50 (Adult & Youth)
 OMSI boasts the U.S.S. Blueback as part of its permanent collection. The Blueback is the last non-nuclear, fast attack submarine that was built by the U.S. Navy and had 31 years of active service. Tours are available daily.

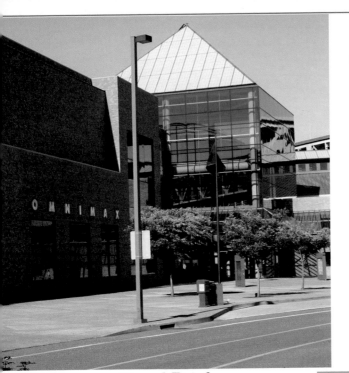

OMSI

Oregon Museum of Science
and Industry
1945 SE Water Avenue
1.800.955.OMSI (6674)
503.797.4000
Hours:
Mid-Sept. to Mid-June
9:30 a.m. to 5:30 p.m.
Closed Mondays

Mid-June to Mid-Sept.
(Summer)
9:30 a.m. to 7:00 p.m.
Open daily
Time Allotment:
3-6 Hours

Travel Brief:

Located at the south end of the Eastbank Esplanade, OMSI is accessible by foot, bike, car or bus from the heart of Portland. As Portland's science center, OMSI is a must-see destination.

Since 1944, OMSI has stimulated the imagination of children and adults through unique and interactive, hands-on educational exhibits. As one of the top 10 science museums in the country, it is a world-class attraction that offers an entertaining and educational experience for the entire family. Its 219,000 square feet contain five exhibit halls, eight science labs, an OMNIMAX® Dome Theater, Oregon's largest planetarium and the U.S.S. Blueback.

www.omsi.edu

TAG™ Tip: Museum Combo (admission, OMNIMAX movie, and choice of planetarium or submarine tour): Adult-$19 Youth-$15

Admission:
Adult - $9
Youth/Senior- $7
(3-13 and over 63)
(Prices and schedules are subject to change.)

Unique Sight Features of the Eastbank Esplanade

The Stackstalk: This is a hybrid beacon-part masthead, part wheat stem, part smokestack. Made of rolled steel tubes and a stainless steel basket, it thrusts a Japanese glass fishing float in the sky.

The Ghost Ship: This grand lantern marks the river's current edge, made of copperplate, copper bar, a stainless steel substructure, and fitted with hundreds of prismatic pieces of art glass.

The Echo Gate: The sculpture echoes the long gone pier buildings in Portland. It is an orphaned doorway that suggests passage but no destination. It is made of copper plate, heat-formed, fitted and welded.

The Alluvial Wall: Clinging to a concrete retaining wall, it alludes to the layers of the river, denoting the pre-industrial geology; a blend of sedimentation and erosion form cold-forged steel plates with bronze castings between its layers.

Eastbank Esplanade: Vera Katz

Completed in 2002
**Time Allotment:
1-2 Hours**

Travel Brief:

The Eastbank Esplanade is one of the newest attractions to Portland. Completed in 2002, it is a mile and a half of paved pathway that extends from the Hawthorne Bridge to the Steel Bridge, and connects OMSI with the Rose Quarter.

On any day, the Esplanade hosts a multitude of outdoor activities, from a simple stroll to an invigorating run or bike ride. The trail can be used in conjunction with Waterfront Park to create a unique three mile loop of urban trail in the heart of Portland.

With 280 trees and 43,695 shrubs that are all native to Oregon, the Esplanade helps each of us learn a little more about our natural habitat. Multiple sign posts will guide you through the features of the walkway. Keep in mind this park was constructed to improve the natural habitat for fish and wildlife, as well as provide recreational space for citizens, which makes it an exceptional urban space.

Unique features of the Esplanade include a 1,200 foot floating walkway, which is the longest of its kind in the United States and four unique pieces of public art: The Echo Gate, The Ghost Ship, The Stackstalk, and the Alluvial Wall.

★ The Echo Gate
★ The Ghost Ship
★ The Stackstalk
★ The Alluvial Wall
★ Floating Walkway

Rose Quarter

Time Allotment:
1 Hour

Travel Brief:
The premier sports complex of Portland, Oregon. This facility contains both the Memorial Coliseum and the Rose Garden on 38 acres.

In 2005, several big-ticket concerts played the Rose Garden, including Neil Diamond, Paul McCartney, and U2.

The Rose Garden is Portland's crown jewel, as a sports and concert venue it seats approximately 20,000. Opened in 1995 as a multi-purpose arena that gives the Portland Trail Blazers their renowned home court advantage, it will play host to a new National Lacrosse League expansion team in 2006.

Tickets are available through Ticketmaster Outlets.
503.224.4400

Portland's Memorial Coliseum stands as a tribute to the veterans of war and has a 12,000 seat capacity. This stadium opened in 1960 and served as the original home of the NBA's Trail Blazers. The Portland Winter Hawks (WHL Hockey) still play a number of games in the facility. In addition, this space also accommodates over 40,000 square feet of exhibit halls.

NE Larrabee
NE Weidler
NE Broadway
Broadway Bridge
Winning Way
Memorial Coliseum
Rose Quarter
Rose Garden Arena
N Interstate
N Vancouver
Steel Bridge
N
MAX Lines

Oregon Convention Center

777 NE MLK Jr. Blvd.
503.235.7575
800.791.2250
Time Allotment:
1 Hour

Travel Brief:

Opened in 1990, with a half million square feet of space, and enlarged to over a million square feet in 2003, the Oregon Convention Center is most recognizable for its twin green, glass towers that grace Portland's skyline.

Situated just to the Southeast of the Rose Quarter, the convention center (the largest in the Pacific Northwest) hosts some of the region's largest events.

This building was built to keep Oregon beautiful. It is an energy-efficient facility; incorporating abundant lighting, the placement of a "white roof" to meet state standards for heat abatement, and one of the largest and most extensive storm water management systems for a building of its size. The notion of creating a huge building that leaves a small environmental footprint is unique to Oregon, and is being emulated in other similar construction projects worldwide.

The Oregon Convention Center contains a public art collection worth upwards of $2 million. Take a walk through the lobby and bask in the light, ambiance, and beauty of a unique building that is unlike any similar sized space in the country.

www.oregoncc.org

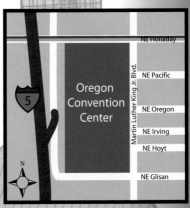

NE Holladay
NE Pacific
Martin Luther King Jr. Blvd.
Oregon Convention Center
NE Oregon
NE Irving
NE Hoyt
NE Glisan
5
N

Extras

Chapter 5:

Downtown Portland

B

NORTH WATERFRONT

BRIDGES	MILES		BRIDGES	MILES
MORRISON	.3		BROADWAY	1.4
BURNSIDE	.6		FREMONT	1.9
STEEL	.9		KITTRIDGE	4.6

PORTLAND GENERAL ELECTRIC

Calendar of Events:

For complete listing of events: www.travelportland.com or Visitors Information Center at Pioneer Square

January:
New Year's Eve Celebration (Pioneer Courthouse Square, page 20)

February:
Portland International Film Festival: 503.221.1156

March:
St. Patick's Day Festival (Selected areas such as: Kell's & Paddy's)

Spring Beer and Wine Festival (Oregon Convention Center, page 63)

April:
Qing Ming Festival (Portland Classical Chinese Garden, page 44)

City of Portland Chess Tournament (Pioneer Courthouse Square, page 20)

Portland Beavers Baseball (PGE Park, see page 37) through September

Portland Timbers Soccer (PGE Park, see page 37) through September

May:
Cinco de Mayo Celebration: 503.232.7550 (Waterfront Park, page 24)

Rhododendron Show (Crystal Springs Rhode Gardens, Eastmoreland, 503.777.1734)

Zoo's Gone Wild Spring Break Party (Oregon Zoo, 503.220.3687)

June:
Portland Rose Festival: 503.227.2681 or www.rosefestival.org

Portland Arts Festival: 503.227.2681 (South Park Blocks, page 31, PSU, page 32)

Wells Fargo Summer Concert Series (Oregon Zoo, 503.220.3687) through August

International Children's Day (Portland Classical Chinese Garden, page 44)

Festival of Flowers (Pioneer Courthouse Square, page 20)

July:
4th of July Celebration & Fireworks (Waterfront Park, page 24)

Waterfront Blues Festival: 503.973.3378 (Waterfront Park, page 24)

Group Health Seattle to Portland Classic (STP): 206.522.3222 Starts in Seattle

Noon Tunes (Pioneer Courthouse Square, page 20) through August

Portland International Beer Festival: portland-beerfest.com (North Park Blocks, page 47)

Oregon Brewers Festival: 503.778.5917 (Waterfront Park, page 24)

Yoshida's Sand in the City (Pioneer Courthouse Square, page 20)

Live after 5 Summer Blues Concert Series (Pioneer Courthouse Square, page 20)

Hood to Coast: 503.292.4626 (Start at Mount Hood)

August:
Mount Hood Jazz Festival: 503.491.5950 (Gresham)

The Bite of Oregon: 503.248.0600 (Waterfront Park, page 24)

Festa Italiana: 503.665.4723 (Pioneer Courthouse Square, page 20)

India Festival (Pioneer Courthouse Square, page 20)

Lebanese Festival (1820 SE 16th Ave) More Info: www.zoobiz.com/events

Providence Bridge Pedal: 503.281.9198 (Waterfront Park, page 24)

Monthly Art Walks:

- Every first Thursday of the Month:
  Shops and art galleries in the Pearl and Downtown are
  open late and feature newly exhibited artwork.
- Every first Friday of the Month:
  Features shops and galleries in Multnomah Village that
  exhibit unique arts and crafts.
- Every last Thursday of the Month on North Alberta Street:
  Features shops, galleries and restaurants stay open late.
  It is great for exploring arts, crafts and cuisine.

Calendar of Events: Continued from Page 66

September:

Art in the Pearl: 503.722.9017 (North Park Blocks, page 47)

Race for the Cure: 503.553.3680

October:

Greek Festival: 503.234.0468 (Holy Trinity Greek Orthadox Church)

Halloween at the Oregon Zoo: 503.220.3687

Portland Marathon: 503.226.1111 (Start & Finish: Plaza Blocks, page 28)

Oktoberfest (Oaks Park, 503.233.5777)

November:

Christmas Festival of Lights (The Grotto: 503.254.7371) through December

December:

Holiday Ale Festival: 503.252.9899 (Pioneer Courthouse Square, page 20)

Christmas Festival of Lights (The Grotto, 503.254.7371)

Zoo Lights (Oregon Zoo, 503.220.3687)

Holiday Decorations (Pittock Mansion, 503.823.3624)

*Phone numbers provided inside the brackets are for the locations. All other numbers are for the event.

Pearl Parks:

Admissions: None

<u>3 hours suggested</u>

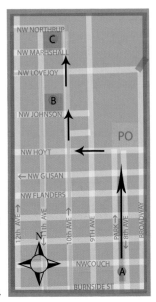

A) Start at the Bronze Elephants (page 46) that mark the entrance to the North Park Blocks (page 47) and stroll north.

B) Walk west (away from the river) on NW Hoyt Street. Take a right on 10th to Jamison Square (Page 52).

C) Continue north along 10th Ave to Tanner Springs (Page 53).

To extend the tour: Catch the streetcar to Northwest Portland (page 54/55) and spend the rest of the day shopping.

Central City: Arts and Parks

Admission: Portland Art Museum and Oregon Historical Society

<u>1/2 to a full day suggested</u>

A) Begin at Portland State University (Page 32/33) and walk north through the South Park Blocks (Page 31).

B) Stop at either the Portland Art Museum (page 34), Oregon Historical Society (page 35), or both.

C) Continue north to Pioneer Square (page 20 to 22).

To extend the tour: Walk east toward the Willamette River. Spend your remaining time exploring Waterfront Park (page 24).

Walking Tours

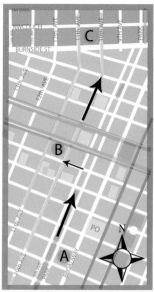

Historical, Literary Tour:

Admission: Oregon Historical Society

<u>3 hours suggested</u>

    A) Begin the day with a scholarly look at Oregon's history at the Historical Society (page 35).

    B) Walk north along the South Park Blocks (page 31) to Historic Multnomah County Central Library (page 36) built in 1913.

    C) Take the streetcar (page 10) to Powell's Bookstore (page 48/49).

To extend the tour: Finish with purchasing a rare or new book at Powell's. Relax with a cup of coffee or tea in the Brewery Blocks or Pearl District (page 50).

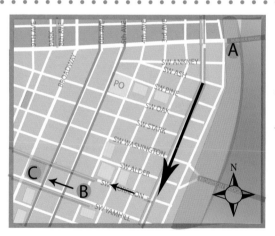

Saturday/Sunday Shopping and Sights:

Admissions: None

<u>1/2 to a full day suggested</u>

A) Start at Portland's Saturday Market and Skidmore Fountain (pages 42/43). Purchase local hand crafted goods that are great for gifts and as unique souvenirs.

B) Jump on the MAX Train (page 8/9) to Pioneer Place (page 23) and immerse yourself in the fashion and style of shops like Saks Fifth Ave, and Tiffany's Co.

C) Stroll down Morrison Street towards Pioneer Square (pages 20-23) and Nordstroms to complete a full day of shopping and gift hunting.

Downtown by Rail: Structured around streetcar accessibly.
Admissions: Portland Art Museum, Oregon Historical Society
Full day suggested

A. Start at Portland State University (Hatfield School of Government Building) (pages 33/34)- Located at the intersection of the Streetcar, Fareless Square and the University District. Board the streetcar.

B. De-board the streetcar and tour the Portland Art Museum (page 34).

C. Walk across the South Park Blocks (page 31) to the Oregon Historical Society (page 35).

D. Walk or take the streetcar to Powell's Bookstore (page 48)

E. The streetcar (page 10) will take you to Northwest where you can stroll boutique shops. Re-board the streetcar to the MAX (page 8/9)

F. Walk or take the MAX at Pioneer Place (page 23).

G. Stroll the art galleries in downtown Portland near Pioneer Place: Gottlieb Gallery, Froelick Gallery, Augen Gallery, and Broderick Gallery are all located between 1st and 3rd Ave between Yamhill and Taylor Street.

H. End the day at the Oregon Sports Hall of Fame. It is located on Salmon Street adjacent to the Plaza Blocks (page 28/29).

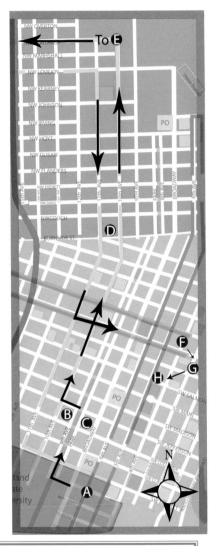

TAG™ Tip: Don't forget your umbrella. Though tours are structured to keep you as warm and dry as possible, walking outside is still necessary to get from one place to another.

Walking Tours

River Loop:
Admissions: OMSI, Oregon Maritime Museum

<u>3 to 6 hours suggested</u>

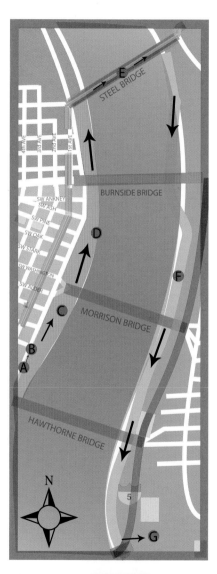

A. Start at Salmon Street Springs (page 27) and head north along Waterfront Park (page 24/25).

B. Take a look at the world's smallest park 'Mill Ends Park' (page 26) in the middle of Naito Parkway at Taylor street and continue to head north towards the glass pillars of the Convention Center (page 63) across the river.

C. Waterfront Park will take you past the Founders Stone, the Battleship Oregon Memorial, and the Japanese American Historical Plaza.

D. Stop at the Oregon Maritime Museum.

E. Cross the river on the Pedestrian Walkway at the Steel Bridge linking Waterfront Park to the Eastbank Esplanade (page 60/61).

F. Walk south on the Esplanade for some of the best views of the Portland's skyline.

G. End the journey at OMSI (page 58/59). OMSI may extend the tour to an entire day.

Fountains of Portland

The Benson Bubblers

In 1912, Simon Benson (a lumberman and civic leader) commissioned 20 drinking fountains with a $10,000 gift. He wanted to offer loggers something other than beer to quench their thirst. Benson once said that after the fountains were installed, saloon sales decreased 40%. The first Benson Bubbler was installed at SW Fifth and Washington. A. E. Doyle, architect of the Multnomah County Library and the Meier & Frank Building, designed the graceful bronze four-bowls. By 1917, the city had installed 40 fountains - known as Benson Bubblers - throughout downtown. When running freely, four-bowls use less than four gallons of water per minute. There are now 52 Benson Bubblers. The fountains flow freely from 5 a.m. to 10 p.m. daily.

In 1896, the Portland Water Committee began a tradition of providing free water for public drinking fountains. For decades travel writers called Portland's free-flowing fountains symbols of hospitality and abundance. The 128 drinking fountains throughout Portland include 75 single-bowl variations of the Benson Bubbler.

There are three, four-bowl fountains in front of Keller Auditorium on SW Third, SW Front and SW Ankeny which are similar to the Benson Bubblers but of a slightly different design. Nellie Robinson, the donor, gave $2,000 for these fountains when she died in 1921.

Fountain Tour

Numbers correspond to the list on the next page.

1. Skidmore Fountain: SW Burnside & Ankeny, 1st & Front
For more information see page 42.

2. The Kelly Fountain: SW 6th & Pine
Water flows over 20-foot steel shapes and was designed by Lee Kelly, one of Portland's most prolific artists. Installed in 1977.

3. Commonwealth Fountain: SW 6th & Stark
Carter, Hull, Nishita, McCulley and Baxter designed this fountain. It captures the feel of a mountain stream on a busy sidewalk. Installed in 1977.

4. O'Bryant Square Fountain: SW Park & Stark
"A Fountain For A Rose," was a gift from Donald Card Sloan, a Royal Rosarian. The inscription reads "May you find peace in this garden." Installed in 1973, it was designed by Danile, Mann, Johnson and Mendenhall.

5. Pioneer Courthouse Square Waterfall Fountain:
SW Broadway between Yamhill & Morrison
For more information see page 20.

6. Animals in Pools:
SW Yamhill & Morrison between SW 5th & 6th
Ten fountains with 25 bronze sculptures of Pacific Northwest animals. Installed in 1986 for the Local Improvement District for the MAX light rail. Designed by Georgia Gerber.

7. The Bath Tub: SW 6th between Yamhill & Taylor
This granite fountain features a painted aluminum sculpture by artist Robert Maki. The fountain was installed in 1977. Water flows slowly over the rounded edges reflecting the urban movement around it.

8. Rebecca At The Well/Shemanski Fountain:
SW Salmon & Main on SW Park
For more information see page 31.

9. Keller Fountain: SW 3rd & 4th and Market & Clay
For more information see page 30.

10. Elk Fountain: SW Main between 3rd & 4th
For more information see page 28.

11. Salmon Street Springs: SW Salmon at Waterfront Park
For more information see page 27.

The Willamette River

Sternwheeler Rose:

This charming vessel is a wonderful and informal way to view the City of Portland. Boarding at OMSI (page 58) both Bunch and Dinner Cruises are available. The cost ranges from $28 to $38 per person and is also available for private charters.
Call to confirm availability and times:
503.286.7673
www.sternwheelerrose.com

The Portland Spirit:

Enjoy fresh Northwest cuisine, live entertainment and a spectacular view of the City. The Portland Spirit is the perfect place to take out-of-town guests or celebrate special occasions. Reservations are recommended for lunch, brunch, dinner or event cruises.
503.224.3900; toll-free 800.224.3901
www.portlandspirit.com

Columbia River Adventures:

The Outrageous, Portland's high-speed jetboat provides scenic excursions to the majestic Columbia Gorge, historic Astoria, Oregon and the Willamette River. Box lunches and onboard beverage service are available at additional cost. Reservations are recommended.
503.224.3900; toll-free 800.224.3901
www.outrageousjetboat.com

Willamette Jetboat Excursions:

Experience spectacular sights and the heart stopping excitement on the Willamette River on a high speed jetboat. Trips are daily and reservations are highly encouraged.
503.231.1532; toll-free 888.538.2628
www.willamettejet.com

Recommended Restaurants

Lunch Suggestions:
Downtown:
Red Coach 615 SW Broadway 227.4840

Traditional hamburgers.

Café Voila 901 SW Washington 595.5606

New York style deli and coffee shop with a Portland twist. Good for a quick bite.

Good Dog/Bad Dog 708 SW Alder 222.3410

Hot dogs of all shapes and sizes.

Paddy's Bar and Grill 65 SW Yamhill St. 224.5626

An Irish style pub with a unique liquor display.

Pearl & Nobb Hill:
Kornblats Delicatessen 628 NW 23rd Ave. 242.0055

New York style deli serving delicious sandwiches to rich cheesecake.

Alexis Restaurant 215 W Burnside St. 224.8577

Great authentic Greek food.

OBA! 555 NW 12th Ave. 228.6161

Unique Latin style food that hits the spot, awesome dessert!

Dinner Suggestions:
Downtown:
Huber's 411 SW 3rd Ave. 228.5686

Turkey everyday, every hour. One of the oldest restaurants in Portland and serves a great Spanish coffee.

Portland City Grill 111 SW 5th Ave. 450.0030

The best view in town! Upscale Pacific-Rim cuisine.

Mother's Bistro and Bar 409 SW 2nd Ave. 464.1122

Traditional comfort food with lots of flavor! Dumplings, pot roast and biscuits are some local favorites.

Fernando's Hideaway 824 SW 1st Ave. 248.4709

Spanish Tapas. Great for a full meal or a quick snack.

El Gaucho 319 SW Broadway 227.8794

Provides an excellent selection of carnivorous options.

Pearl & Nobb Hill:
Andina 1314 NW Glisan St. 228.9535

Peruvian food with a twist. Cool, upscale & well worth a stop.

Bluehour 250 NW 13th Ave. 226.3394

Trendy dining spot with a great Happy Hour. Definitely try the fondue.

Performing Arts Venues:

New Theater Building:
1111 SW Broadway
Portland, OR 97205
The New Theater Building is
Portland's newest performing arts
center. It features two theaters
(Winningstad and Newmark)
that provide an intimate theater
experience.
Features: Winningstad–Seats 292
Newmark- Seats 916
Entrance on Broadway

Keller Auditorium:
222 SW Clay
Portland, OR 97201
This theater, originally known
as the Civic Auditorium, was
built in 1917 and renovated in
1978. Acting as the primary
theater for the city of Portland,
the Keller Auditorium hosts
numerous performing arts
events each year.
Features: Seats 2,992
Main Entrance on Third[rd] St.

Arlene Schnitzer Concert Hall:
1037 SW Broadway
Portland, OR 97205
A traditional concert hall that originally
opened in 1928 and was restored to its
present condition in 1984. Visitors are
greeted by a 65 foot high "Portland"
sign above SW Broadway. This marque
contains approximately 6,000 lights.
Features: Seats 2,776
Orchestra Pit: 15 musicians
Entrance on Broadway & Park

An Evening Out

Travel Brief:

Portland Center for the Performing Arts is the place to receive information and assistance in navigating Portland's theater community.

Portland has multiple venues which include the Arlene Schnitzer Concert Hall, Keller Auditorium and the New Theater Building (Newmark Theater, Dolores Winningstad Theater and Brunish Hall). Both the Schnitzer Concert Hall and New Theater share Main Street and Broadway.
Performing Arts Information:
503.248.4335 General Information
503.432.2917 Box Office

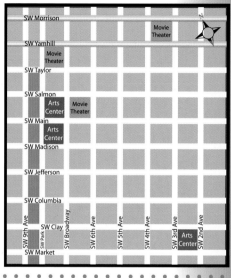

Movie Theaters

Regal Fox Tower 10

846 SW Park Ave.
Portland, OR 97205
800.326.3264
Admission:
Adult Matinee: $6.50
Child/Senior: $6.00
Adult: $9.00

Regal Broadway Metro 4

1000 SW Broadway
Portland, OR 97205
800.326.3264
Admission:
Adult Matinee: $6.00
Child/Senior: $5.25
Adult: $8.25

Regal Pioneer Place Stadium 6

340 SW Morrison
Portland, OR 97204
800.326.3264
Admission:
Adult Matinee: $6.50
Child/Senior: $6.00
Adult: $9.00

Regional Map

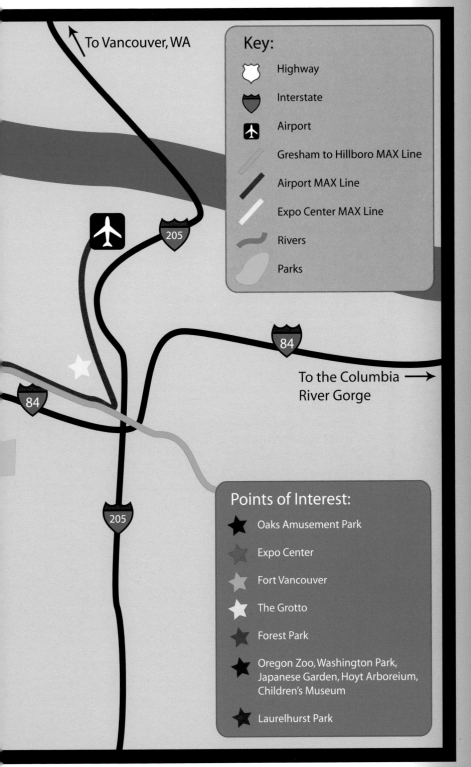

To Vancouver, WA

Key:
- Highway
- Interstate
- Airport
- Gresham to Hillboro MAX Line
- Airport MAX Line
- Expo Center MAX Line
- Rivers
- Parks

84

To the Columbia River Gorge →

205

Points of Interest:
- Oaks Amusement Park
- Expo Center
- Fort Vancouver
- The Grotto
- Forest Park
- Oregon Zoo, Washington Park, Japanese Garden, Hoyt Arboreium, Children's Museum
- Laurelhurst Park

Index:

Map Index: